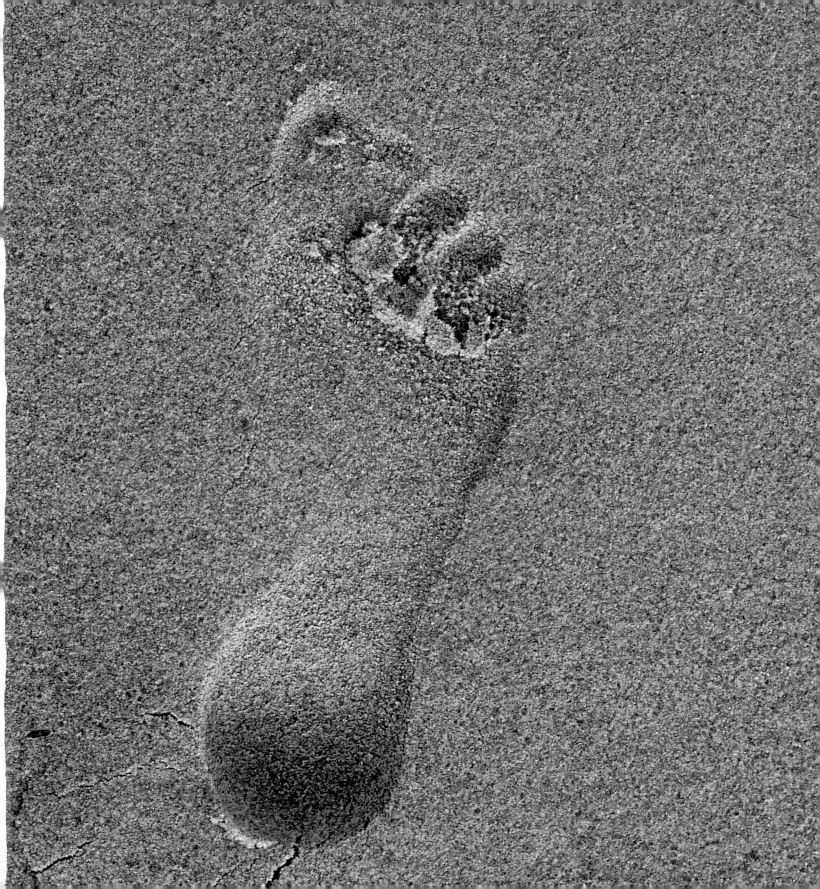

STAFFORD CLIFF

THE WAY WE LIVE

by the sea

WITH 256 COLOUR PHOTOGRAPHS BY

GILLES DE CHABANEIX

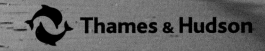

Thames & Hudson

THE WAY WE LIVE
by the sea

INTRODUCTION

Footprints in the sand, emblematic of our love affair with the shoreline; distant figures at the sea's edge; a child's swing on a tropical island against impossible blues of sea and sky; small boats moored in a working harbour, their painted surfaces gleaming in the coastal light; a decorative day-bed beneath an awning, creating a scene of voluptuous luxury by the Indian Ocean; azure colours around a Pacific atoll; and calm waters, combined with a temple, in a scene of the utmost serenity and tranquillity: all these potent images evoke the enchantment of being and living by the sea. People will never cease to be drawn to coastal areas, invigorated by the sheer energy of the water or calmed by the movement of the tides. And then there are the simple, seductive experiences to be enjoyed: stepping out in the early morning to walk barefoot in the sand; picking up an unusual seashell, smooth pebble, or a handful of driftwood; the luxury of a candle-lit picnic on the beach at dusk; a wedding ceremony on the seashore.

From coastal hamlet or summer villa retreat above the azure waters of the Mediterranean or Caribbean, to lonely waterfront outposts on the edge of the Atlantic Ocean, the diverse pleasures of living by the sea are almost invariably accompanied by a sense of well-being, of a freshness in life. Those of us who select a life by water may still choose from lake, river or seaside locations and the different lifestyles they dictate. In this book, many of the homes and hotels illustrated were clearly intended to be places of pure escape. Isolated cottages, villas with verandas and terraces looking out to the ocean, apartments in sea-front towns, individualized hotel units. They all constitute tempting alternatives to the pressures of city life. The photographs in this book by the late Gilles de Chabaneix evoke the experience of living and staying by the sea in locations around the world. Their variety is considerable; their common factor is that they are all alluring.

Part of the attraction of the coast is undoubtedly the quality of light; it has a luminosity which never occurs inland. We have all seen the extraordinary effects of light on the sea, even on grey, misty days: the burning midday glare, or the spectacular beauty of a sunset, or a glancing ray of sunlight illuminating a patch of ocean on a dark, stormy afternoon. Such elements have been the inspiration for countless painters and composers.

What might be called the folk memories of seafront life have distinct national differences. In the United Kingdom, for instance, these are bound up with the tradition of the annual exodus from the inland towns and cities to the coast, later supplanted by the package holiday abroad. Nevertheless, in spite of changing habits, the image of the British seaside of sand castles, donkey rides, Punch and Judy shows, remains deeply embedded in the national consciousness – a vestigial recollection of a time when factories closed down for one or two weeks and whole populations moved to the coast. When foreign travel became an option for many people, it was still to the sea they headed, though Blackpool and Morecambe were now replaced by Mykonos and Mallorca – or even Sri Lanka and Mauritius, both of which feature in the pages which follow.

In the United States, the seaside meant many things, but one abiding image is that of the Gatsby-like lifestyle of the rich and famous of the eastern seaboard. The older money gathered around Newport, Rhode Island, while the ritzier media crowd spread to the Hamptons and Fire Island. On the west coast, Malibu and Venice became the quintessential expressions of Los Angeles by the sea, while the fashionable people of San Francisco bought houseboats across the bridge in up-market Sausalito. In the meantime, the Florida coast became synonymous with 'retirement'.

On the continent, especially in France, the development of any part of the coast as a fashionable place to be was often artist-led. We see the Normandy coastline through the eyes of Boudin and Monet. Gauguin brought light and colour to Brittany; and, later, the Fauves settled around pretty little Collioure on the south-western Vermilion Coast.

But appreciation of the light and colours of the coast is as much a state of mind as a question of specific location. The qualities of seashore life have been recreated in many a city apartment or house, far from the coast, through the use of colours, textures and materials, drawn from living by or on the sea: shades of blue, green and white; sand, bleached wood, rattan, shells, scrubbed stone, pebbles; clean, simple surfaces devoid of pattern, timber cladding, domestic areas reflecting light, frosted glass. All such elements can come together to constitute a reminder of our fascination with life at the edge of the ocean.

The appropriate use of materials in coastal architecture and design is a recurrent theme in the pages which follow, especially in relation to a new generation of hotels. Where once resorts were made up of houses, villas, high-rise complexes – not specifically different from buildings inland – the last decade or so has seen the emergence of a more environmentally friendly style of construction. Resorts in places as far apart as Kenya, Thailand, Bali and Tahiti have adapted local styles of building, using immediately available 'natural' materials to create luxury accommodation, so completely integrated into the surrounding environment as to be scarcely noticeable.

This new seaside style, evidenced in hotel design and the booming market in beach properties, is informed with a spirit which is both primitive yet intensely modern. Instead of replicating all the air-conditioned conveniences of city life, it embraces the simple and the basic: furniture made from driftwood; a shower installed under a tree; the lazy elegance of hammocks; cooking and eating outside, sleeping on the sand. Accompanying this spirit is a taste for the renovation of such buildings as abandoned boat-sheds, light-houses or fishing shacks; this lifestyle is typified here by a surfer's hut on a Mexican beach, looking almost as though it had been washed up by the sea.

Such are some of the current expressions of what it means to live by the sea – basic materials, simple amenities, pared-down decoration, uncomplicated expectations, befitting exposure to the raw energy of the ocean. Whether you live in a city flat, a town house or an industrial loft, far from the shore, these photographs prove that, in the end, it is not a matter of travel, not about summer holidays or long-haul flights. It is the inspirational qualities of this new spirit which are the subject-matter of this book – the passion for the shoreline, the beach, the coast, the water, the harbour, and the architecture and artefacts that accompany them. In other words, a sea-view – a refreshingly simple solution to a less complicated way of life.

Preceding pages
A startling expression of the
consciousness of life by the sea: take
a day-bed, covered in materials
conventionally intended for interior
use, and place it on a beach beneath a
semi-transparent canopy in colours
which seem strangely reflective of
those of the landscape and seascape.

The interaction of ocean waters with
other natural phenomena – reefs, the
level of the seabed, islands – produce
colour effects of often unexpected
beauty, especially when viewed from
the air: here, a sandbank in the
waters of the Great Barrier Reef
(*opposite* and *right*) provides the
ultimate in isolation – no deckchairs,
no people, no intrusive noise, just
the means of escape when you've had
enough.

The oceans and seas of the world are
capable of wreaking terrible havoc;
but when calm, they can induce
a feeling of palpable serenity – the
ideal surroundings for a temple.

A small building on a promontory
of the Cycladic island of Serifos fits
organically into the coastal terrain.

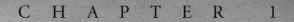

SEASIDE ARCHITECTURE

Houses, Cabins, New Developments

Water has always been an important adjunct to buildings, intensifying their presence and impact. And the wider expanse of the ocean, in whatever climate, seems to inspire generosity and ingenuity in design and construction.

The word 'seaside' has many connotations, most of which involve an architectural component. From cabins and beach-huts at popular resorts or pavilions hidden among the tropical foliage of some Pacific island, from new 'natural' hotel developments to converted lighthouses or sea defences, from Mediterranean cliffside villages to Thai temples on the water, there is an immediate excitement about the style, colour and structure of waterfront buildings around the world. The variety in the types of coastal buildings represented on the following pages entails a lifetime of choices. All of them evoke the pleasures of living by the side of the ocean in locations around the world and, in their different ways, are all enticing.

Preceding pages
The striking red spire of a white
church rises above the tropical
vegetation on this stretch of the coast
of Bora-Bora in the Tahitian
archipelago, again making the
connection between an architectural
expression of spirituality and the sea.

Whatever the latitude, communities by the sea – and a good proportion of the world's population does live on the shores of its oceans – enjoy a quality of light quite unlike that of inland towns and cities. It seems more luminous, more vibrant, and somehow more pure. Both the relaxed beach-front of Salvador di Bahia (*opposite*) and the more stern, workaday waterfront of a small Norwegian town (*above*) are made attractive and engaging in environments of variegated blues.

Very different forms of community and location are defined by their position on the sea. The island of Patmos (*left above*), famous for its Christian heritage and its majestic fortress-monastery, stands out in pristine white against the unbelievable blue of the Aegean. Whole cities, too, like Cape Town (*left below*) take on new and exciting dimensions by having a waterfront from which the varied sounds and activities of the sea can mingle with the more familiar ones of the city.

Inevitably, a position on the sea informs the lives and development of the communities there, whether large cities like Marseilles (*right above*) or more modest towns like Salinas (*right below*). Fishing will almost certainly figure largely in local life; and, in the case of Marseilles, shipping and maritime activity drove the growth and expansion of the city. It also occupies a uniquely picturesque site on the Mediterranean.

Seascape, landscape and architecture: the almost organic combination of these three elements lends a unique quality to certain communities by the sea. The Cycladic island of Santorini (*left above*) is one of the most remarkable sights in the Mediterranean, where the white and blue houses of its two main communities are gathered above the remains of one of the greatest volcanic explosions in history. Not quite as dramatic, but nevertheless utterly at home in their environment, the villas of Amalfi (*left below*) ascend the headlands above the Gulf of Salerno. A similar stacking above the seafront makes a particularly pleasing arrangement of Italianate neoclassical villas on the island of Symi in the Dodecanese group in the Aegean Sea (*opposite*).

The enrichment of the presence of the sea in the form of a waterfront is amply visible in the form of a small, decorative Scottish coastal town (*left above*). The same marvellous excitement produced by the proximity of the sea or ocean also lends a particular quality to the great Australian city of Sydney (*left below*), where dockside warehouses have been transformed into cafés and hotels.

Similar settlements in the Comoros (*right above*) – plain, local villages – and in Sicily (*right below*) derive an additional dimension from their position on the water – certainly, one which is denied to their inland counterparts.

An integral part of a settlement on the water, unless it is for leisure purposes alone, is the working harbour. On the Île de Ré (*above*) pleasure and working craft combine to create a centre of activity in the local community. Traditional harbours, too, always seem to have a beneficial effect on the quality of waterfront architecture.

As in many parts of northern
Europe, there is a sturdy,
straightforward, but still elegant
quality about the houses
surrounding a fishing harbour in
Scotland (*above*).

More of the architectural pleasures of waterfront life present themselves in the form of the multi-storeyed villas of Istanbul (*left above*). More prosaic, but still impressive, is the quayside market building on the coast near Edinburgh (*left below*).

Is there some strange quality about waterfronts and harbours which universally attracts a robust style of architecture with strong graphic definition? Certainly, these two examples lie very far apart: the Venice lagoon (*right above*); a row of shops bordering a harbour in Scotland (*right below*).

Hydra, in the Argo-Saronic grouping of islands in the Aegean Sea, is almost everything one could hope for in the civilized settlement of mankind by the sea (*left*). Once the setting for a Sophia Loren film (*Boy on a Dolphin*), it probably still looks as it did one hundred years ago. In contrast to such architectural sophistication, this artist's house in Corsica (*opposite*) – home to someone who creates sculpted furniture from driftwood – seems almost to spring from the materials of the local coastline.

Preceding pages
More an expression of man stepping
into the sea than simply settling
beside it, the beach-hut, a largely
Victorian invention, permitted a
suitable degree of modesty on entry
into the water. These examples create
a rather touching effect under a
lowering Normandy sky.

What began as a simple adjunct to the new fashion of bathing in the sea has now become a much sought-after addition to beach life. These huts in Cape Town (*opposite* and *above*) are equipped with every type of convenience to make a day at the seaside a close replica of a day at home. In the United Kingdom alone there are more than nine thousand huts dotted around the coastline.

Overleaf left
A dwelling at the water's edge exercises a peculiar fascination, harking back perhaps, to a primitive stage of human occupation of the land. This simple structure, near Cape Town, looks lost and vulnerable against the adjacent mass of water.

Overleaf right
A modern take on the traditional architecture of Mykonos enjoys a position by the Aegean.

Clearly conceived as the simplest of
dwellings by their owners, these
isolated cottages, near Cape Town
(*opposite*) and on the island of Jersey
(*above*), represent a tempting
alternative to city life. Both examples
have a robustness of construction,
almost as though their original
builders had intended them to
withstand any threat from the
elements.

Crouching amid the local flora, the raw architecture of this solitary structure (*left*) on a rugged stretch of coastline near Cape Town looks pleasantly weathered in the salt air. The metal roof and timber walls have a rudimentary quality, in strict contrast to the sophistication of this island retreat (*opposite*).

Situated above the crystal-clear waters around fashionable St. Barthélemy in the Caribbean, this private holiday villa (*right*) looks out to sea. The intense light, reflected from the smooth surface of the water, illuminates this very stylish home, complete with pool, deck, hot tub and loungers: a place for total peace and relaxation.

Certain materials and forms have a
peculiar appropriateness to a life
close to the sea. Clapboard, notably,
has a way of looking entirely at home
as cladding for seaside housing, as in
this famous example: Prospect
Cottage (*above*), formerly the home
of the late Derek Jarman, artist and
film-maker. The garden, too,
contains many references to the sea
in the form of shingle, driftwood
and found objects, picked up on the
shore at Dungeness.

The clapboard houses of the tropical North Queensland coast are often raised on stilts to permit the free circulation of air beneath the floors (*above*). In this instance, a wooden picket fence makes a perfect companion.

Overleaf
Long, low houses, especially with verandas, also seem to fit the seashore environment, especially those subject to strong winds.

Relatively simple, low construction seems a perfect approach to the design of a house by water, like this example in Brittany (*opposite*). Twenty-six miles north of Tahiti lies the atoll of Tetiaroa, once the private retreat of Marlon Brando. The house (*above*), with its gingerbread-style wooden trims along the veranda, is dwarfed by the tropical palms, which act as a natural windbreak.

One step further from the solitary dwelling by the water's side is the structure which is actually extended into the sea, whether for religious, personal or strictly functional reasons. Walkways and platforms (of which the seaside pier is only a massive enlargement) have a curiously hypnotic effect, leading the eye to anticipate and the feet to explore – a Buddhist shrine in Thailand (*opposite*); a fishing cabin in Chile (*left above*); and a lifeboat station in Wales (*right above*).

The crystal-clear lagoon of Tetiaroa, the unique atoll of the Society Islands, is encircled by thirteen white-sand islets, ideal places for extending private habitations into the water (*opposite*). Not far away, the small island of Bora-Bora has seen some interesting and sophisticated development in hotel design, whereby accommodation is decentralized and individualized in the form of isolated units built out over the sea (*right above* and *below*).

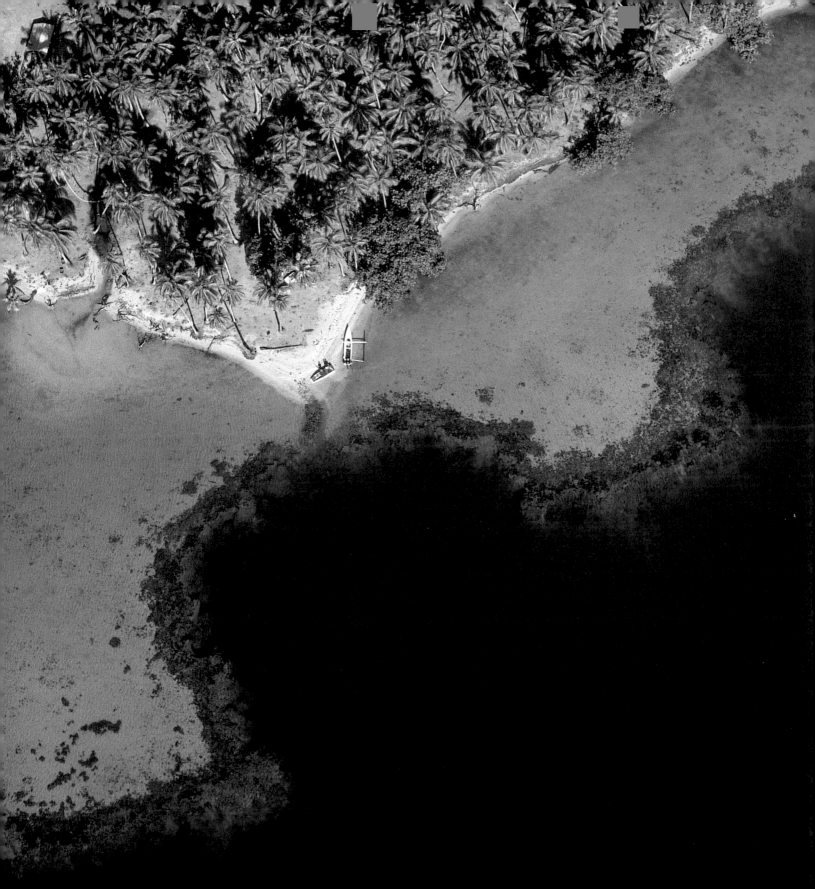

The privacy of a coral island; there are very few marks of human occupation around the glorious waters of Tetiaroa (*opposite*). More emphatic in its imposition of the human imprint on life by the sea is this lagoon resort on Bora-Bora (*right*). In many ways, this simple, timeless, yet utterly sophisticated structure typifies modern developments in hotel design in warmer regions. It uses local materials and building styles to create accommodation which reflects and respects indigenous skills and cultures, but still provides all the luxuries demanded by today's holiday-makers.

Overleaf
There is a very special quality to life on an island, especially on a relatively small islet: there are the strong feelings of apartness and isolation, but also the sense of being in touch with and at the mercy of the larger forces of nature, of which the background sounds of the sea provide a constant reminder. Islands, like this resort off the coast of Mauritius, also provide a sense of adventure, of being apart from the crowd – an agreeable sensation in the era of mass-tourism. And, of course, there is always the enticing possibility of buying one's own island as a secret hideaway.

Preceding pages
Surrounded by the sea, but not very far from the southern shore of Sri Lanka, the tiny private islet of Taprobane makes a marvellously secluded setting for an exclusive resort hotel. Within the encircling trees, the building unfolds its architectural elegance (*p.94*).

Another aspect of man's interaction with the sea and coastline, sometimes forgotten or underestimated, is much more utilitarian than many of the examples we have seen on preceding pages. There is a whole category of buildings, including lighthouses, watchtowers, forts and lookouts, which are now occasionally being taken up for conversion to exciting shoreline residences. These examples, however, still serve their original purpose: on the island of Jersey (*above* and *below left*); at Salinas, Mexico, (*opposite*).

This lighthouse (*left*) on the Île de Ré, western France, makes an odd companion for the formal, terraced housing on either side of it.

The presence of the sea, or at least large expanses of water, almost inevitably attracts the building of lookouts and balconies – a response to the urge to gaze out beyond the shoreline: in Chile (*left above*); on the Île de Ré (*right above*).

The planting of a parasol – here, by the Venice lagoon – is an accompaniment to establishing a presence on the seashore.

CHAPTER 2
THE EXTENDED ASPECT

Terraces, Decking, Jetties, Platforms, Private Beaches

Humankind's fascination with the shoreline naturally translates into a design vocabulary of structures to enhance the feeling of being close to the sea. In this chapter there are gardens which open out on to the beach, boardwalks which reach down to the shore, terraces which give the illusion of stretching out over the sea. From the Great Barrier Reef to the French Riviera, terraces, decks and viewing points are an essential adjunct to the urge to spend time at the edge of the ocean. Note how many of the examples illustrated demonstrate a willingness among contemporary designers and architects to employ forms and materials which fit seamlessly with their surroundings; and sometimes all that is necessary to enjoy the setting is a hammock slung between two trees, or a palm-thatch roof and a few chairs.

Opening up contact with the shoreline can take many and varied forms, simple and complex. A garden on the Irish coast (*left above*) gives on to the water's edge by means of a 'thirties design 'sunburst' gate – itself a symbol of opening up to worlds beyond. Much more elaborate as a way of approaching the sea is this exotically planted and landscaped coastal garden at Hammamet, Tunisia (*left below*). A boardwalk suffices for access to this stretch of coastline, near Cape Town (*opposite*).

The strict modernist lines and colour schemes of the interior of this house on the coast of Devon (*above*) have been extended to the exterior above the shore. A small terrace and a single chair make a simple statement about our fascination with looking out to sea.

Again, the simplest of arrangements
on a terrace overlooking the
Mediterranean at Nice (*above*); the
presence of the sea enlivens and
lightens both interiors and exteriors.
This terrace, additionally, gives the
illusion of being immediately above
the water.

The simplest of materials and
forms combine to give this hotel
terrace in Queensland, Australia,
an understated elegance as well as a
marvellous view out to sea (*above*).
Robust hardwood furniture looks
especially appropriate in this setting.

Everything about this terrace overlooking the Mediterranean on the French Riviera looks exactly fitting and in context (*above*). It is secluded, yet offers a view of the sea on three sides; it is straightforward, yet the dominant materials of cane and terracotta have been made to be set in the sun and by the sea.

Halfway between private and
public worlds, the terrace provides
a tranquil place for eating
and drinking, reflection and
contemplation. This example on
the island of Madeira (*above*) has
the obvious advantage of being
completely open to the sea and sky.
Chequered paving and cane
furniture complete an idyllic scene.

Again, on the island of Madeira, this variation on the terrace theme creates a very different effect (*above*). Instead of recognizing the sea as an all-important surround, the sheltered nature of this arrangement succeeds in framing it as a backdrop to the enjoyment of a meal within.

The two seating areas illustrated here, complete with colonial-style furniture – in Mauritius (*left above*), and in Sri Lanka (*left below*) – beautifully demonstrate the joys of the seaside terrace or veranda. In warm climates such adjuncts to the house really do serve as substantial additional rooms, while the presence of the ocean background enlivens and lightens the shaded parts.

The maritime allusions are clear in the construction of this patio directly above the sea (*opposite*) on the island of Madeira. Its form is that of a ship's prow, while its surface suggests a pattern of pebbles.

An effective seating area, however, does not necessarily require an elaborately constructed and furnished terrace, veranda or loggia. Sometimes a simple stretch of decking, accompanied perhaps by a parasol or awning, can be an effective but informal way of creating a space for the enjoyment of sun and sea air. An important aspect of this outside dining and sitting area on the Île de Ré (*above*) is its use of furniture in materials sympathetic to the environment.

In the relaxed atmosphere of life on the tiny Pacific island of Bora-Bora, it has not even been necessary to lay down decking or, indeed, to erect anything beyond a very simple shelter, to create an area of warmth and conviviality (*above*). All that has been necessary to create this shoreline idyll has been the placing of a table and a few chairs beneath a roof made of local materials.

The reassuringly simple yet elegant forms of loungers are an essential accompaniment to lazy days by the beach: on Lizard Island, Queensland (*left*); and on the Tahitian island of Bora-Bora (*opposite*).

Overleaf
A modern interpretation of traditional Balinese architecture characterizes the Aman Resorts group of hotels on the Indonesian islands. Here it lends lends grace notes to the spectacular setting of the Amankila ('peaceful hill') resort near Manggio, east Bali. Beyond lie magnificent sea and coastal views.

This resort on Lizard Island, on the Great Barrier Reef (*left above* and *below*), is typical of a certain type of modern seashore hotel development. Its materials and colours show sensitivity to the local environment, while offering great comfort in rugged surroundings.

The Lizard Island resort (*right*), like many contemporary hotel developments, offers the opportunity of dwelling in a private paradise, within reach of spectacular white beaches. Located right on the Great Barrier Reef, the surrounding seascape reveals itself to the carefully placed viewing points.

It is not just the activities normally associated with days by the sea which are enhanced by the presence of the water. Even the prospect of a game of pool at the Lizard Island resort (*opposite*) appears more enticing against a background of shoreline and boats. And the pleasures of eating at the water's edge have been fully recognized in this hotel on Bora-Bora (*above*); the table is given importance by the decking.

Few experiences are more immediately restful than swinging in a hammock to the sound of the nearby sea. Perhaps partly because of its naval association, it does seem an entirely appropriate adjunct to beach and shore life – here, on Bora-Bora (*above*) and in a resort in North Queensland (*opposite left* and *right*).

Overleaf
This resort on Kiwayu island, on Kenya's east coast, makes a virtue out of using local materials and building styles in the construction of its very private 'bandas' (homes). Each hammock-strung veranda is totally secluded, yet only a few metres from the water's edge.

Natural-looking materials and
colours and the continuity of
interior and exterior make this house
at Zihuatenejo (*above*), on the
Pacific coast of Mexico, very much
part of the local seashore
environment.

The extended terrace, with pool, of the same Zihuatenejo house (*above*) continues the use of very natural building materials, especially in the roofing and its supports. Rough brickwork and terracotta tiles reinforce the impression that the house is almost an organic part of the Pacific coastline.

All these examples from around the world of terraces looking out to sea draw part of their charm from the character of their furniture, although this takes many different forms: cane for a Mauritian house (*left above*); hardwood on Bali (*right above*); canvas and wood on Bora-Bora (*left opposite*); and rattan on a Kenyan veranda (*right opposite*).

As a substantial architectural adjunct to a larger house or hotel, a veranda constitutes a remarkably flexible space in accommodating all the activities of the good life – eating, drinking and conversation. At the same time, its openness, especially when looking out to the sea, introduces visual drama and exciting variations of light to the whole setting. This example, attached to a hotel retreat just off the coast of Sri Lanka (*pp. 58–59*) (*above*), makes great play with the effect of columns, both structural and purely decorative.

On a cliff-top near Monte Carlo, this
terrace-cum-pergola (*above*)
provides the owners of the house
with a year-round dining area and
views over the sea.

The decorative terrace of this
seashore house on the island of
Mauritius is clearly an integral part
of the whole building. Yet, at the
same time, through its contact with
the local plant and avian life, it acts
as a transitional space, bringing the
experience of living by the sea into
the house.

Low tide changes the mood induced
by this sea view and reveals the
evocative shapes and colours of
beached fishing vessels.

CHAPTER 3
SEASIDE COLOURS & MATERIALS

Whites, Blues, Greens, Wood, Stone, Glass

The interiors of houses by the sea, wherever they are located, often seem to have a design vocabulary in common. Colours tend to be light and reflective, although some examples here opt for dark brown, as though re-interpreting the interior of a well-appointed boat or ship. Blue and white is a combination which seems to have a universal 'coastal' feel, from the Greek islands to Goa. Certain materials, too, seem curiously appropriate to life with nautical overtones, like the painted panelling common to several houses on the Île de Ré illustrated here. And even in houses and apartments inland, such materials and forms may invoke the resonances of seaside dwelling: ship-shape storage systems; porthole-like windows; translucent blinds. One of the most interesting features of this chapter is the illustration of 'buildings' at the Kenyan resort of Kiwayu, where local 'natural' materials are used to create individualized accommodation in traditional styles.

Preceding pages
A house by the sea – or, even better, on an island – is one solution to the need to escape increasingly crowded and cramped urban centres, to find space and enjoy the special luminosity of light from the ocean. The owners of this house on the Île de Ré, off the west coast of France, have sought a kind of maritime simplicity in this panelled interior, illuminated by the fresh island light, suggesting a casual lifestyle.

Left
White painted panelling in the dining-room, coupled with neat storage units, gives this Île de Ré house a maritime feel.

Looking at the interiors of the Île de Ré house, it seems almost possible to speak of a distinct 'seaside style', characterized by simple forms and materials, and a distinct colour range. Nor is this 'style' solely confined to seashore or island living. This London apartment (*right*), for instance, utilizes uncovered floor-boards, a light palette, cotton covers, and opaque perspex shutters to achieve a very similar look, almost as though 'seaside' is as much a state of mind and choice as a location.

Again, in a London house, this kitchen (*left*) makes copious use of tongue-and-groove boards and white tiles to achieve a light, airy feel. Neat storage units, transparent storage jars and rudimentary light fittings somehow hint at things nautical. The purple-grey of the allium plants completes a distinctly seashore palette. Overall, there is an avoidance of unnecessary pattern and decoration.

This interior of a house on the Tunisian coast (*left*) has all the freshness and airiness we associate with being close to the sea. The overall white colour scheme throws the rough wood of the tree trunk and the wall carving into sharp relief.

Reflective surfaces and large areas of white help to enhance the effects of the island light in this kitchen (*right*) of a house on the Île de Ré.

There is an unfussed quality about
this kitchen, again in a house on the
Île de Ré (*above*), in its simple lines,
white walls and cupboards. The
timber-clad ceiling evokes beach-hut
construction, while the large window
allows light to flood the space. What
could have been the darkening effect
of the relatively low ceiling has been
countered by the overall white
colour scheme. A painting on the
wall of men in a boat reinforces the
generally nautical look of the room.

This bathroom in a London house (*above*) is a good example of how materials, colours and design can evoke the feeling of freshness and openness normally associated with life on the coast or even at sea. The ample light from the window is reflected from the polished wooden floor – there is an urge to kick off your shoes and walk barefoot. The timber cladding around the bath and lower walls, the outdoor folding chair and wooden duck-board all carry nautical undertones.

There are several features of this modernist house on the Devon coast (*left*) which, in addition to its actual location, purvey the feeling of seaside living. Furniture, for instance, is fairly minimal, and the tile floors remain unadorned. The stair rails, too, look as though they could have been designed for a boat.

Though far removed from the sea, this house in Carpentras (*right*) has many of the characteristics of freshness and freedom we associate with a coastal dwelling. The choice of furnishings is eclectic, but it has resulted in an entirely pleasing and workmanlike domestic environment. Much of the furniture has been made to the owner's design in relatively inexpensive materials. Other items have either been recovered from salvage shops, like the 1940 architect's lamp, or bought from household goods chain-stores. And the table setting is dominated by a boat-like candle-holder. The folding and stacking chairs could serve equally well outside the house.

SEASIDE COLOURS & MATERIALS

Light colours, enlivened with bold
splashes, and robust, open furniture
set the tone of this bedroom (*right*)
in an Île de Ré house. Such touches
as the rough floor tiles, the slatted
table and the open metal chair have
more than a suggestion of the
outside about them, of life on the
island and closeness to the sea.

It is scarcely surprising that a grey/blue palette should be associated with life by the sea, since convention sees them as the colours of the very water itself – here, seen from the shores of the Île de Ré (*right above*). The fading blue of a door on that island (*left above*) could almost be taken as a reflection of the sea nearby.

116

The smooth and the rough of seaside style; this Mexico City hotel (*left above*) has adopted a décor and watery colour scheme distinctly suggestive of an on-board lifestyle. Bleached, washed-up pieces of wood represent another aspect of the sea life (*right above*), but equally can be put to good use in the home and garden, either as ornament or as part of other structures or furniture.

Cool blue-greys and whites seem an entirely appropriate choice for the decoration of the bedroom in a house on the Corsican shore (*opposite*). Similar tones, with several maritime references (ship-in-bottle and sextant) draw attention to the sailing traditions of the Morbihan *département* of Brittany, a land where association with the sea is inescapable (*right*).

The bathroom of this modernist Devon house (*left*) picks up and continues the 'ship' and 'sea' themes of the other rooms. Ultramarine, mingled with transparent elements, dictates the overall appearance, while the other details, notably the lights, have a distinctly nautical air.

The colour blue always seems associated with life by the sea; it seems especially appropriate, then, that it is the dominant colour in the bedroom in an Île de Ré house (*right*).

Overleaf
Colours really do seem to achieve a greater intensity through the action of ocean light, whether applied by man or those of nature: contrasting blues on a façade at Key West, Florida (*p. 124*); luxuriant planting in a Moroccan garden (*p. 125*).

The combination of blue and white in building and materials brings a freshness and brightness, suggestive of the sea itself, to decorative schemes of coastal communities around the world. The blue of a painted door in a house in Hammamet, Tunisia, introduces a coolness to the interior hall.

On the Aegean island of Santorini the whole colour scheme of the local domestic architecture is blue and white.

The startling blue on the façade of this building in Goa darkens in the shadows cast by the afternoon sun. Intricate palm-tree motifs in the arched windows evoke visions of a tropical seaside paradise.

Blue and white stripes – material always somehow suggestive of deck-chairs – provide an apt background to this vacation scene on the veranda of a Mauritian villa (*left*).

Blue is everywhere on Cycladic Santorini – outlining doors and windows, applied to tables and chairs, and generally making a dramatic splash against the white pozzuolana of the houses (*right*).

Overleaf
The kitchen/diner of a house in Santiago, Chile, has carried the blue and white combination to the extreme of including the floor in it. Neat storage units and a nautical-looking light fitting complete an ensemble where the owner seems to have tried deliberately to create the fresh, bright feel of seashore style.

The outlining of apertures, especially in blue, is a decorative mannerism which can be seen throughout the Mediterranean; this particular example (*opposite*) is on a house on the island of Ibiza. An interior variation on the style has been neatly applied to the bathroom of a house on the Île de Ré (*right*).

Just as certain colours seem automatically to associate themselves with coastal living, so too do forms and materials. Panelling, for instance, constantly appears in seaside and island houses: in Tahiti (*left above*) and in Morea (*right above*), where the rough wood seems to have been bleached by the sea. In an Irish house (*left opposite*), there are additional references to fishing and the nautical life. On the Île de Ré, in the house of a distinguished French designer (*right opposite*), an unusual reference to the sea forms a highly sculptural ornament: a section of a whale's backbone.

The veranda of this Tahitian house (*above*) converts easily to a substantial extra 'room', with the aid of seaside-style blinds.

A rough-cast storage unit makes a
powerful impression in a Corsican
house (*above*). The wicker baskets,
neatly labelled, look oddly
reminiscent of luggage prepared for
a lengthy sea voyage.

References to the sea-going life abound in this interior of a house in the Morbihan *département* of Brittany (*left*), appropriately enough since this coastal region boasts a long and vigorous maritime heritage. Particularly striking here are the simulated portholes and the boat-shaped light fittings.

Again, porthole-like windows dominate this Bora-Bora interior (*above*), full of allusions to the life of the shore. A collection of sea trophies is displayed on rough-cast shelving, itself reminiscent of underwater formations. The table top is seemingly set with pebbles, while the banquette seating suggests that of a boat.

Straightforward forms and materials give all these interiors a distinctly 'seaside cottage' feel, occasionally enlivened by a direct reference to the nautical life: in Tahiti (*left above*); on the Brittany coast (*right above* and *left opposite*); and in Corsica (*right opposite*).

The town of Essaouira, on Morocco's Atlantic coast, is a place of fine traditional houses. Opting for elegant simplicity, the owners of this particular example have succeeded in creating an especially pleasant domestic environment. Natural-looking fabrics, bold arch forms, plain white walls (*above*), and exposed wood, rattan furniture and straw mats (*opposite*) emphasize a sense of openness and freshness, all illuminated by the coastal light.

Overleaf
The fittings and colours of this bathroom in a house on the Île de Ré suggest those aboard an ocean liner. In the same house (*following pages*), a bedroom continues the sea-going feel in the panelled walls, totally appropriate to an island home.

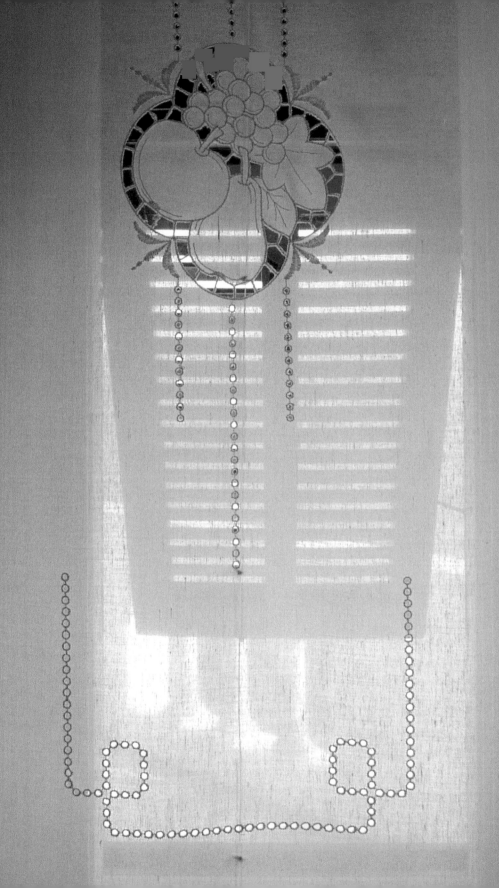

Preceding pages
A tented pavilion in a hideaway hotel complex on the Indonesian island of Moyo is a fine example of new trends in luxury lodging by the sea, whereby local, natural materials are used to create structures very much at one with the surrounding environment. Canvas and cotton in loose, draped forms cover the furniture or act as blinds, in contrast to the dark, rich browns of the indigenous hardwoods. Windows on both sides give the space a decidedly boat-like feel, akin to that of a traditional island steamer.

The exceptional intensity of light by the sea, especially in warm climates, will often call for some form of filtering to preserve the shade of an interior in welcome contrast to the fierce brightness outside: in a Monte Carlo apartment (*opposite*); mosquito nets forming elegant shapes, as well as being functional, on Bora-Bora (*above*).

SEASIDE COLOURS & MATERIALS

The supreme luxury of very simple things is marvellously evident in the separate 'houses' of the Kiwayu safari resort on an island just off the coast of Kenya (*right*). Typical of many new hotel developments which show special sensitivity to the local environment in warmer climates, each unit is constructed with a palm-thatch roof and a matting floor. The king-size bed is transformed into a private space by the turquoise mosquito net.

Perhaps the purest expression in these pages of seashore dwelling: this surfer's cabin (*above* and *right*) at Todos Santos, Mexico, has all the casualness and arbitrary quality of the beach itself, while the structure looks almost as though it has been washed up by the sea. Two chairs look out to the ocean, presumably waiting for the right kind of wave.

The bedroom of the surfer's hut (*preceding pages*) exhibits the engaging thrown-together qualities of the overall structure, a feature which extends to a very eclectic array of bed linen (*above*). The grand pretensions of a four-poster bed are here adapted to become a frame for mosquito netting.

A slightly more formal simplicity in beach dwelling is expressed by the coloured beaded curtain in this relaxed setting on Mauritius (*above*).

The 'natural' look of the main living structures of the safari resort on Kiwayu island is carried through to the fittings of the interiors (*left*), employing local weaves and materials under the palm-thatch roof, backed by a hanging piece of contemporary fabric.

Each unit within the hotel complex on Kiwayu has a degree of individuality (*right*). Even the hanging closets, though all in local traditional materials, are differentiated from each other; some examples have their own canopy covers.

SEASIDE COLOURS & MATERIALS

Bold use of local building and furnishing materials and fabrics characterizes this simple dwelling on the Mexican Pacific coast (*right*). The overhanging roof provides shade and some protection from the outside heat, but substantial openings in the walls still allow plenty of light to flood into the interior. Note the ocean shore allusion in the ring of pebbles embedded in the painted floor around the small occasional table.

A similar approach to hotel planning to that on Kiwayu – namely, the creation of separate units furnished with local materials and artefacts – characterizes this complex on the island of Tahiti (*above* and *opposite*). Once again, traditional indigenous building methods , employing bamboo and palm leaves, have been used to create a light, airy environment.

This scene of the sea off the coast of Japan magnificently conveys a sense of the ocean's immensity and bounty.

CHAPTER 4
WASHED UP

Flotsam, Shells, Rocks, Pebbles, Fruits of the Sea

The sea itself provides a fascinating range of forms and artifacts to embellish the interiors of the preceding chapter. One enterprising artist, for instance, creates fantasy furniture-sculpture from driftwood gathered from the beaches of Corsica. Shells, pebbles and coral have long been recognized as having great decorative and display qualities, although acquiring them in the present day should only be done with proper regard for the conservation requirements of maritime environments. Certain forms, such as pebbles, also inspire the design of exterior and interior surfaces, notably the extraordinary rooms created by Gio Ponti for the Parco dei Principi hotel in Sorrento. And, finally, there are the fruits of the sea: gastronomic delights and marvellous visual displays in quayside markets.

Garnered from the Corsican beaches, driftwood is the raw material which one island dweller has employed to create an extraordinary series of furniture-sculptures (*preceding pages* and *left*). These pieces are so full of fantasy in their form, so expressive of natural forces, that they almost seem to have been tangled together by the sea itself.

The phantasmagorical forms of the 'tables' and 'chairs', thus created from driftwood, embody the principles of chance in that their shape and construction is entirely dependent on what pieces are washed up and on their creator's vision (*right*).

The metamorphosis of sea-washed objects: ocean-side dwellers have a ready-made store of natural materials – driftwood, shells and pebbles – at their front door. Whether used for construction, decoration or as pure ornament, their textures, colours and shapes are often varied and inspiring. The rough, vertical lines and textures of a cabin on Bora-Bora (*left above*) and the smoother, horizontal patchwork of wood which forms the walls of this house on Morea (*left below*) are ingenious examples of building with found materials. Yet another driftwood furniture-sculpture at the house in Corsica (*opposite*) has a strangely numinous quality when placed beside a small shrine.

The very special textures and colours of sea-washed driftwood make the exterior and interior of this island home doubly decorative (*left* and *right above*). Smooth panelling on the ceiling is in stark contrast to the rough, faded qualities of the walls. A stylishly posed paddle makes another sea reference.

Driftwood and whalebone have been combined to make this highly original table in the Kiwayu island hotel complex (*left above*). An extraordinarily expressive section of sea-washed wood becomes an impromptu sculpture in an Irish coastal home (*right above*).

Overleaf
Fragments of coral and shells form a cabinet of curiosities in a Bora-Bora house. Nowadays, though, concern for the protection of the marine environment makes the formation of such collections well nigh impossible.

179

Shells and starfish combine with paintings and ceramics in a chest-top display in an Île de Ré house (*left above*). The separate units of the same Kenyan hotel complex are all embellished with arrangements which allude to the place's seashore location (*right above*).

Another example of decorative ingenuity at Kiwayu: this time, the smaller shells are displayed in a large conch shell (*left above*). Shells are an important element in this miniature cabinet of curiosities in a house on Key West, Florida (*right above*).

In a fascinating house, built of local materials, on the island of Sumbawa, east of Bali and Lombok, an artist who works almost entirely in wood has created marvellous and strange articles of furniture, drawing on the local skills of carving from wood. As ornament there he has created a number of arrangements, including this one of a variety of shells and, most interestingly, the sea-washed back-bone of a turtle (*left*). The decorative arrangements, utilizing the fruits of the sea at Kiwayu, are also applied to candlelight on the beach (*opposite*).

A collection of nineteenth-century shell furniture and decoration (*left* and *opposite*) makes for a startling domestic environment in this house on the island of Jersey. Such plundering of the resources of sea and shore would now be regarded as unacceptable.

The walls and stepways of a garden in Madeira (*opposite*) provide an extraordinary example of the graphic possibilities of shell shapes, used in any position. One famous house in Mexico City, that of the painter Frida Kahlo, has one façade embellished with conch shells embedded in the wall (*right*).

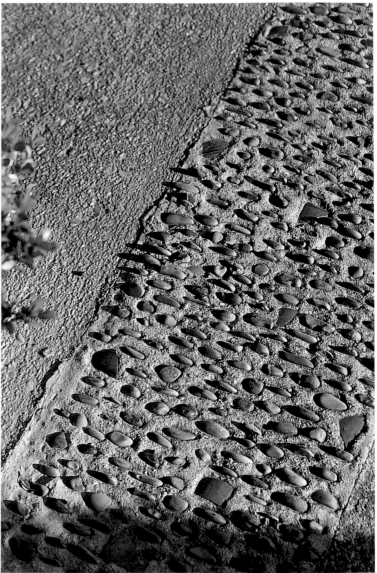

These examples of decorative pebblework are drawn from both coastal and inland houses and gardens (*above*, *opposite* and *overleaf*). Yet, our reaction to all of them, whatever their location, is touched by pleasant memories of the shoreline and the sea.

The imaginative, graphic use of pebbles chosen specifically for their colour and shape can achieve quite amazing dramatic effects as paving or flooring. On the Cycladic island of Santorini such arrangements have pretty well achieved the status of folk art (*left* and *right above*, *left opposite*). In contrast to the intense, mosaic-like working of the Greek designs is the sophisticated simplicity of an amusing figure in pebbles from the Bahamas (*right opposite*).

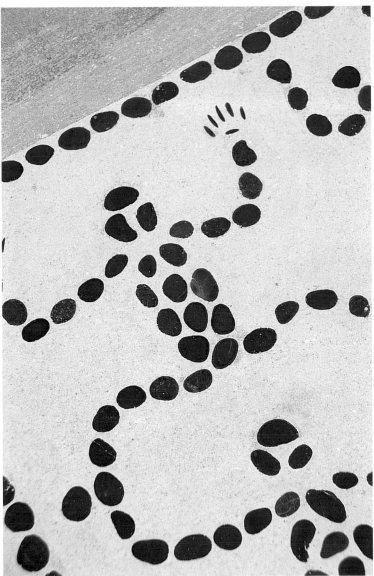

Overleaf
The interiors of Gio Ponti's Parco dei Principi hotel in Sorrento take up the pebble theme in a particularly imaginative way. Many interior walls are covered in ceramic 'pebbles', glazed blue or white, reflecting the colours of the Mediterranean in an overall grotto effect.

Bringing the local shoreline into the interior: the owners of this house on the Île de Ré have incorporated locally found pebbles as intriguing linear designs in the paved floors (*opposite* and *right*).

The cool, rough texture of pebbles or stone slabs in houses in warm climates brings welcome relief underfoot from the heat outside; it seems peculiarly appropriate in bathrooms: on the Île de Ré (*left above*); on Tahiti (*right above*). In this house on the island of Mallorca the kitchen floor of closely set pebbles (*opposite*) entirely complements the robust strength and forthrightness of the original structure.

The decorative qualities of boldly
patterned tilework fragments really
do assert themselves in the bright
light of the southern Mediterranean
– in Tunisia (*above*) and in Tangiers
(*opposite*). Even the somewhat
haphazard arrangements in
shoreline houses seem to suggest all
that is arbitrary and unexpected in
the washed-up yield from the sea.

The bounty from the sea and from maritime experience in general, especially that with decorative potential, goes far beyond the scale of pebbles and shells. Half-dismantled boats and fishing nets make large-scale still-lifes in the Comoros (*above left* and *right*). These net buoys on the Irish coast, near Dublin, could certainly bring ornament to any interior (*opposite left*), while an abandoned anchor in Cape Town makes a monumental outside sculpture (*opposite right*).

Preceding pages
The day's catch: the waters around the island resort of Kiwayu, just off the coast of Kenya, abound with all kinds of fish. These include tuna, marlin, sailfish, wahoo and kingfish.

Fresh fish for sale: wooden boxes filled with the catch of the day line the quayside on the Aegean island of Santorini (*left*).

Fish imagery: this carving (*right*) against a net-like background embellishes the exterior of a restaurant in the old port of Marseilles, a graphic reference to that city's long association with all things nautical.

Avoiding the supply chain to supermarket or processed food plant, markets appeal to a deep human wish to acquire raw food in as fresh a condition as possible. And nowhere is this more true than in fish and seafood stalls the world over – here, in Mauritius (*above*) and Marseilles (*opposite*). Quayside displays, especially, delight and inspire by the brilliance of their hues and the boldness of pattern, offering delicious visual preliminaries to the pleasures of cooking and consumption. Pinks and reds combine with silvers to glisten and glow in the rays of a coastal dawn.

WASHED UP

The decoration scheme of this Paris interior is clearly intended to bring the sea into the centre of the city (*right*). Even apart from the fish ornaments, the chairs look as though they have been borrowed from a coastal terrace. The centrepiece, however, is the head sculpture formed from shells, which might have been assembled by a latter-day Arcimboldo.

And then, of course, there is the way that most of us get to experience the sea all the year round – through seafood. Delicious to eat and often fascinating to look at, the fruits of the sea are among the greatest delights of the gastronomic experience (*opposite* and *right*).

A calm sea off the Queensland coast
offers a seductive invitation to the
life afloat.

LIFE AFLOAT

Living with Boats

The enterprising owner of the launch *Eolo* makes a living by conducting tours of the villages and communities of the Venice lagoon. Sprucely presented, the interior and exterior of the craft could serve as metaphors for all that is good about the life afloat. Other images of water-borne elegance are provided by the traditional craft of the Nile, the Indian Ocean and Bali. Such forms, and others, are constantly translated into models and signs, an amazing range of which are illustrated on the following pages.

But perhaps the ultimate expression of shoreline life is a total environment floating on the water, in the form of a complete house or even a house-boat, permanently moored.

LIFE AFLOAT

Rather than being by the water, why not be on the water? The *Eolo* (*right*) is a traditional island craft that sails around Venice's lagoon and its islands, taking visitors to convents, forts, fishing villages, monasteries and other communities.

The *Eolo* somehow serves as a metaphor for all the pleasant aspects of life on the water and the nautical environment. While sailing, its passengers can enjoy the sights around the lagoon and the slightly erie light which comes from the conjunction of sky and water, but its frequent moorings also admit them into a world of pleasurable gastronomy (*left* and *opposite*).

Boat style (*left above* and *below*): the panelled interiors of the *Eolo*, its low-level work surfaces, its ordered cupboards and storage spaces, its seating and the form of the portholes and lighting fittings, all offer distinct inspiration for interior design. Indeed, these forms have already been encountered in houses illustrated in this book (*pp. 138-139*).

The compact work surfaces and gleaming fittings of the galley (*right*) typify the need to maintain order when sailing – in fact, to remain 'ship-shape'.

LIFE AFLOAT

The waterfront of the Aegean island of Hydra probably has not changed much in a hundred years, except perhaps in the restoration and maintenance of the surrounding buildings. But the pleasure craft moored there now far outnumber the fishing vessels (*right*).

The grace of traditional craft: the distinctive form of a felucca's sail creates a graphic image in a Nile sunset (*left above*). Off the coast of Kenya, slim dhows fish the waters around the islands of the Lamu archipelago (*left below*).

These local craft, sailing in the seas around Bali or drawn up on one of that island's superb beaches (*right above* and *below*) have a gracefulness which comes from a fitness for their purpose and an honesty in their construction from locally available materials and the skills of the communities.

The boat form as a metaphor for freshness and freedom is pretty well universal: the sight of raked sails against blue sky or of a prow cutting through the waves immediately evokes that sense of escape to a freer, healthier environment. These model sailboats (*preceding pages*) make an enlivening display in a Tunisian coastal town; a mural in Marseilles suggests the same freshness (*left above*); and the image of a fishing vessel in San Francisco signifies a fish market (*left below*).

A model of a traditional fishing-boat is framed in a structure made entirely of driftwood found on the beaches of Corsica (*right above*). Another, touchingly simple, model boat hangs from a café ceiling on Key West, Florida (*right below*).

At the sign of the boat: in Edinburgh (*left above*); in Barcelona (*right above*); a weather vane in Copenhagen (*left opposite*); on the Île de Ré (*right opposite*).

The fascination which model boats
and ships hold for most people is
very evident in these interiors, made
doubly significant in that they are all
in houses close to the sea: in coastal
Provence (*left above*); and on the Île
de Ré (*right above*, *left* and *right
opposite*).

Everything about these interiors in homes on the Île de Ré suggests life by the sea (*opposite*, *right above* and *below*): wood panelling; model boats and ships; and a nineteenth-century swimming lesson.

LIFE AFLOAT

In addition to the model boat, as
an evocation of the nautical life,
an overall freshness and simplicity
pervades this Île de Ré house (*right*),
in the arrangement of furniture
and the choice of materials, from
the wood ceiling to cotton blinds.
Just visible beyond is the bathroom
previously illustrated (*pp. 144-145*).

LIFE AFLOAT

References to the owner's interest in all things nautical abound throughout this house in Santiago; in this bedroom they take the shape of two particularly elegant models of small boats (*right*).

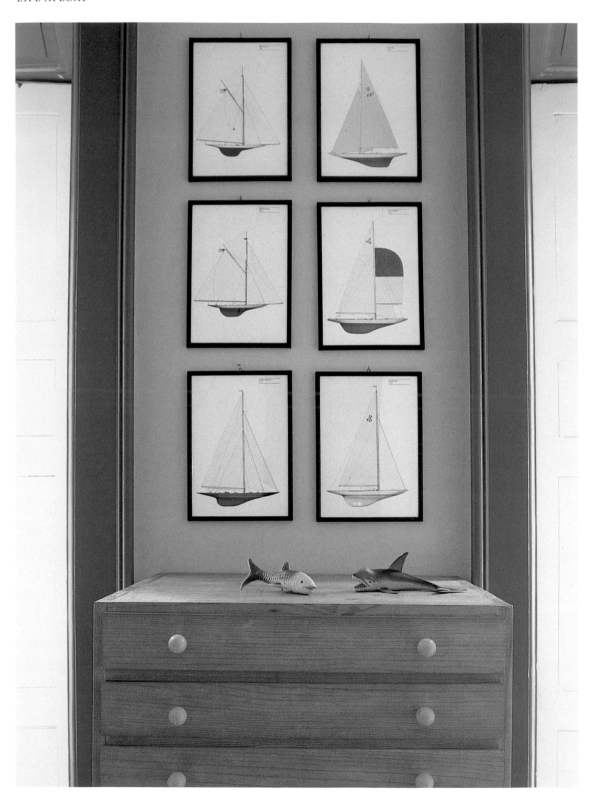

A fine collection of nineteenth-century prints of sailing-boats adorns the bedroom wall of this house on the Île de Ré (*left*). Ceramic fish ornaments complete this nautical display.

This simple bentwood chair (*right*) incorporates an unusual element in the form of a simple model boat: in a house in Naples, one of the great maritime cities of the Mediterranean.

245

LIFE AFLOAT

On the clear blue waters, just off a small island in the Tahitian archipelago, rides perhaps the ultimate expression of what it means to live by the sea: a traditional floating house (*right*).

Simple, elegant solutions to living
right at the sea's edge: these houseboats (*above* and *opposite*) line part
of the waterfront of the fashionable
San Francisco suburb of Sausalito.

Overleaf
The serenity of life by the sea: an invitation in the idyllic form of an elegant Balinese hotel to contemplate the immensity of the ocean.

ACKNOWLEDGMENTS

Designed by Stafford Cliff
Index compiled by Anna Bennett

First published in the United Kingdom in 2006 by Thames & Hudson Ltd,
181A High Holborn
London WC1V 7QX

www.thamesandhudson.com

All photographs
© 2006 Estate of Gilles de Chabaneix

Design and layout
© 2006 Stafford Cliff

Text and captions
© 2006 Thames & Hudson Ltd

The Way We Live: By the Sea
© 2006 Thames & Hudson Ltd, London

British Library Cataloguing-in-Publication Data
A catalogue record for this book is available from the British Library

ISBN 13: 978-0-500-51253-1
ISBN 10: 0-500-51253-1

Printed and bound in Singapore by CS Graphics

The photographs in this book are the result of many years of travelling around the world to carry out commissions for various magazines and clients. Very special thanks is due therefore to all the many people who have helped to make the realization of this project possible, including Martine Albertin, Béatrice Amagat, Catherine Ardouin, Françoise Ayxandri, Marion Bayle, Jean-Pascal Billaud, Anna Bini, Marie-Claire Blanckaert, Barbara Bourgois, Marie-France Boyer, Marianne Chedid, Alexandra D'Arnoux, Catherine de Chabaneix, Jean Demachy, Emmanuel de Toma, Geneviève Dortignac, Jérôme Dumoulin, Marie-Claude Dumoulin, Lydia Fiasoli, Jean-Noel Forestier, Marie Kalt, Françoise Labro, Anne Lefèvre, Hélène Lafforgue, Catherine Laroche, Nathalie Leffol, Blandine Leroy, Marianne Lohse, Chris O'Byrne, Christine Puech, José Postic, Nello Renault, Daniel Rozensztroch, Elisabeth Selse, Suzanne Slesin, Caroline Tiné, Francine Vormèse, Claude Vuillermet, Suzanne Walker, Rosaria Zucconi and Martin Bouazis.

Our thanks also go to those who allowed us access to their houses and apartments: Jean-Marie Amat, Mea Argentieri, Avril, Claire Basler, Bébèche, Luisa Becaria, Dominique Bernard, Dorothée Boissier, Carole Bracq, Susie and Mark Buell, Michel Camus, Laurence Clark, Anita Coppet and Jean-Jacques Driewir, David Cornell, Bertile Cornet, Jane Cumberbatch, Geneviève Cuvelier, Ricardo Dalasi, Anne and Pierre Damour, Catherine Dénoual, Dominique and Pierre Bénard Dépalle, Phillip Dixon, Ann Dong, Patrice Doppelt, Philippe Duboy, Christian Duc, Jan Duclos Maïm, Bernard Dufour, Explora Group, Flemish Primitives, Michèle Fouks, Pierre Fuger, Massimiliano Fuksas, Teresa Fung and Teresa Roviras, Henriette Gaillard, Jean and Isabelle Garçon, John MacGlenaghan, Fiora Gondolfi, Annick Goutal and Alain Meunier, Murielle Grateau, Michel and Christine Guérard, Yves and Michèle Halard, Hotel Le Sénéchal, Hotel Samod Haveli, Anthony Hudson, Ann Huybens, Patrick T'Hoft, Igor and Lili, Michèle Iodice, Paul Jacquette, Hellson, Jolie Kelter and Michael Malcé, Amr Khalil, Dominique Kieffer, Kiwayu Safari Village, Lawrence and William Kriegel, Philippe Labro, Karl Lagerfeld, François Lafanour, Nad Laroche, Rudolph Thomas Leimbacher, Philippe Lévèque and Claude Terrijn, Marion Lesage, Lizard Island Hotel, Luna, Catherine Margaretis, Marongiu, Mathias, Valérie Mazerat and Bernard Ghèzy, Jean-Louis Mennesson, Ilaria Miani, Anna Moï, Leonardo Mondadori, Jacqueline Morabito, Christine Moussière, Paola Navone, Christine Nicaise, Christian Neirynck, Jean Oddes, Catherine Painvin, John Pawson, Christiane Perrochon, Phong Pfeufer, Françoise Pialoux les Terrasses, Alberto Pinto, Stéphane Plassier, Morgan Puett, Bob Ramirez, Riad Dar Amane, Riad Dar Kawa, Yagura Rié, Guillaume Saalburg, Holly Salomon, Jérôme-Abel Séguin, Jocelyne and Jean-Louis Sibuet, Siegrid and her cousins, Valérie Solvi, Tapropane Villa, Patis and Tito Tesoro, Richard Texier, Jérôme Tisné, Doug Tomkins, Anna and Patrice Touron, Christian Tortu, Armand Ventilo, Véronique Vial, Barbara de Vries, Thomas Wegner, Quentin Wilbaux, Catherine Willis.

Thanks are also due to the following magazines for allowing us to include photographs originally published by them: *Architectural Digest* (French Edition), *Atmosphère, Coté Sud, Elle, Elle à Table, Elle Décoration, Elle Décor Italie, Madame Figaro, Maison Française, Marie Claire, Marie Claire Idées, Marie Claire Maison, The World of Interiors.*